D1239571

Being Your Best at Basketball

NEL YOMTOV

Children's Press®
An Imprint of Scholastic Inc.

Content Consultant
Barry Wilner
Associated Press
New York City, New York

Library of Congress Cataloging-in-Publication Data
Names: Yomtov, Nelson.
Title: Being your best at basketball / by Nel Yomtov.
Description: New York : Children's Press, an imprint of Scholastic Inc.,
   2016. | ? 2017. | Series: A True Book | Includes bibliographical
   references and index.
Identifiers: LCCN 2015048506| ISBN 9780531232606 (library binding) | ISBN
   9780531236116 (paperback)
Subjects: LCSH: Basketball—Juvenile literature. |
   Basketball—History—Juvenile literature.
Classification: LCC GV885.1 .Y66 2016 | DDC 796.323—dc23
LC record available at http://lccn.loc.gov/2015048506

Front cover: A basketball player
jumping for a shot

Back cover: A basketball player
preparing to shoot

Find the Truth!

Everything you are about to read is true *except* for one of the sentences on this page.

Which one is **TRUE**?

T or F Basketball is a game played only by tall people.

T or F Basketball is played around the world.

Find the answers in this book.

Contents

THE BIG TRUTH!

The Harlem Globetrotters

Harlem Globetrotters

Basketball player

A referee signaling
a holding foul.

5

The first basketball rules did not say how many players could be on the court.

A group of kids play basketball in Hawaii.

Starting Out

The speed and intensity of basketball captivates people around the world. Millions of men, women, and children in nearly every country play it. Games range from backyard pickup to high-level National Basketball Association (NBA) and Olympic games. Basketball is also a popular sport to watch on television. Audiences in more than 200 countries tune in to the NBA finals each year. If you want to get in on the action, all you need is a desire to have fun and to be the best you can be.

Keeping It Simple

One of the best things about playing basketball is that you don't need a lot of equipment. All you need is a ball, a hoop with a **backboard**, and a smooth floor. You should wear comfortable, loose-fitting clothes. Gym shorts or warm-up pants, and a T-shirt or light sweatshirt are ideal. Wear high-quality, durable footwear with nonskid soles. You'll need them to handle the impact of jumps and quick, sharp changes in direction.

Comfortable clothes

Ball

Nonskid sneakers

Teams often wear matching uniforms.

Whether you have the ball or not, always be ready to take action. You never know when your team may need you.

This Game Is for You

You can develop most of the skills needed to play basketball through practice and training. You will be running forward and backward and doing a lot of jumping as you play. While on the court, be alert and stay focused. Basketball is a team sport, so one of the most important skills is the ability to work well with others. Teamwork is essential—and it will help you be your best.

Many parks and playgrounds have asphalt or concrete basketball courts.

Hit the Court!

An indoor professional basketball court usually has a wood surface. The court measures 94 feet (28.6 meters) long and 50 feet (15 m) wide. High school courts may be shorter in length. The size of outdoor basketball courts can also vary. Outdoor courts are usually made of asphalt or concrete. Those found in schoolyards or playgrounds generally have metal or wooden backboards. Indoor courts have fiberglass or wooden backboards.

Early basketball games used baskets with bottoms that were made to hold peaches.

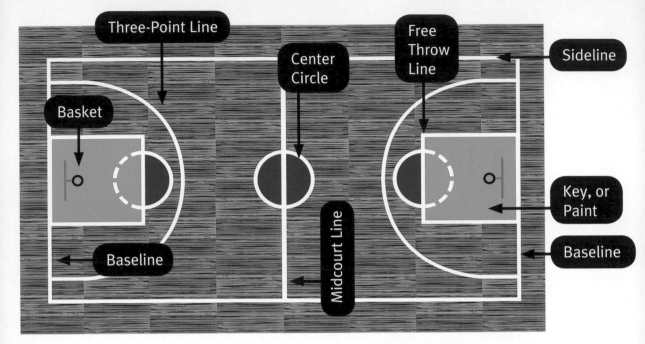

Three-Point Line

Free Throw Line

Center Circle

Sideline

Basket

Key, or Paint

Baseline

Midcourt Line

Baseline

This diagram labels the parts of a standard basketball court.

Court Markings

The midcourt line divides the court into two equal halves. A basket is mounted at the end of each half, with the rim 10 feet (3 m) above the floor. Two sidelines run the length of the court. The baselines run between the sidelines, at the ends of the court. The three-point line is an arc. **Field goals** made from behind this line count as three points. Those made from within it are two points.

The key, sometimes called the paint, is the painted rectangle at each end of the court. The paint on an NBA court is 16 feet (4.9 m) wide. High school and college court paints are narrower by 4 feet (1.2 m). The **free throw** line, or foul line, is at the end of the key opposite the basket. On professional courts, the free throw line is 15 feet (4.6 m) away from the face of the backboard.

Free throw lanes on international courts were shaped differently from other courts until 2010.

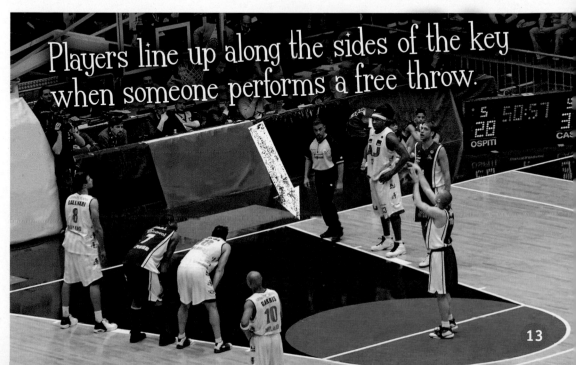

Players line up along the sides of the key when someone performs a free throw.

Kobe Bryant of the Los Angeles Lakers shoots for a three-point basket.

Order on the Court

The object in a game of basketball is to score points by putting the ball through the basket. Teams are awarded one point for successful free throws. They earn two points for field goals made inside the three-point line and three points for shots made from outside it. The team with the most points at the end of the game wins. To make sure game play remains fair, basketball has rules, just like any other game.

An NBA game is 48 minutes long, divided into four 12-minute quarters.

Following the Rules

A player cannot run while holding the ball. He or she has to dribble to move from place to place. If a player stops, he or she must throw the ball within a certain time limit. Referees enforce the rules in a basketball game. They also call time-outs and decide which team has possession of, or holds, the ball once the game begins.

NBA referee Violet Palmer signals the number of a player who committed a foul.

Fouls

The referee calls a **personal foul** to prevent a player from gaining an unfair advantage over an opponent. Personal fouls usually involve physical contact. Pushing, shoving, and tripping are some examples. Charging is a foul that occurs when a player on the offense pushes or runs over a defensive player. Referees sometimes award a fouled player a free throw without any opposing players blocking it.

A player who commits six fouls in an NBA game is ejected.

Fouls such as charging can result in injuries.

When you stop dribbling, you have to pass—fast—to avoid a violation.

Violations

When a player commits a **violation**, his or her team loses possession of the ball. One violation is double dribbling. Players double dribble if they dribble with two hands, or stop dribbling and then start again without anyone else touching the ball. Traveling occurs when a player moves with the ball without dribbling at all. In the NBA, the offensive team is charged with a violation if it fails to shoot the ball within 24 seconds.

Hand Signals

Basketball referees use hand signals to declare that a player has broken a rule. For example, if a player grabs or touches an opponent to stop the person's movement, the player committed a holding foul. The referee grabs his or her own right wrist with the left hand to signal this (left). If two opponents commit fouls against each other at the same time, it's a double foul. The referee crosses both wrists above his or her head (right).

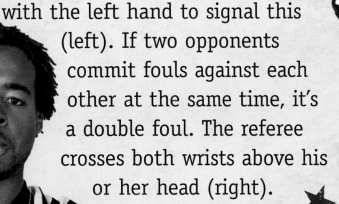

The Harlem Globetrotters

The Harlem Globetrotters combine great on-court skills with comedy and showmanship to entertain their fans.

The team began in 1926 as a serious, all-black squad from Chicago, Illinois. At the time, professional basketball teams only allowed white players. The Globetrotters' games had to be separate events. Globetrotters sometimes played other "barnstorming" teams like them. They also played college teams and, occasionally, professional **league** teams. The Globetrotters won 101 of 117 games played in their first season.

Harlem Globetrotters, ca. 1930

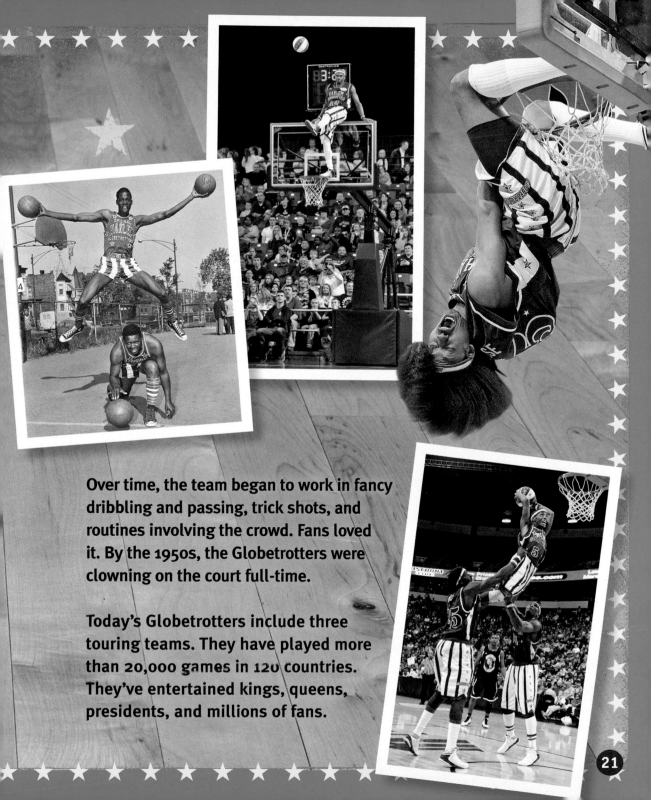

Over time, the team began to work in fancy dribbling and passing, trick shots, and routines involving the crowd. Fans loved it. By the 1950s, the Globetrotters were clowning on the court full-time.

Today's Globetrotters include three touring teams. They have played more than 20,000 games in 120 countries. They've entertained kings, queens, presidents, and millions of fans.

The team with the ball is called the offense. The team trying to prevent the offense from scoring is the defense.

Matee Ajavon with the Atlanta Dream attempts a shot against the Washington Mystics.

All Kinds

Two teams, each with five players, face off
in an official basketball game. Each team
member plays one of three basic positions. The
tallest player is usually the center. Centers are
generally stationed near the basket. The next
tallest players are often the two forwards. They
operate mainly in the corners or on the edges
of the paint. The two guards are frequently the
team's shortest players. Their main job is to
dribble, pass, and shoot.

Combining Skills

Great basketball players go beyond the descriptions of these three traditional positions. In 2012, college student Muthu Alagappan was working at a data **analysis** company. A basketball fan, Alagappan fed information about hundreds of NBA players into the company's computers. He used the resulting analysis to define several new types of player positions. Each type combines the abilities of center, forward, and guard in different ways. Let's take a look at some of these cutting-edge ways to play.

Muthu Alagappan figured out a number of ways some of the new basketball positions might look on the court.

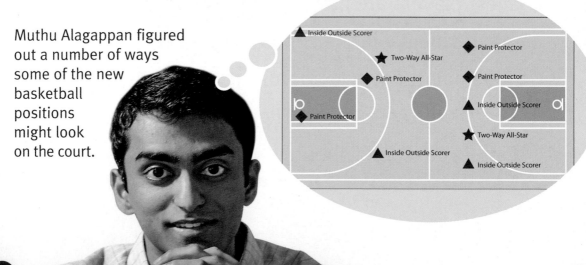

Ball Handlers

An offensive ball handler specializes in dribbling and passing. He or she also excels at attempting many shots and foul shots, or free throws. This player does not often block the opponent's shots. Defenders working against ball handlers are usually skilled at stealing the ball. A shooting ball handler attempts the most shots and usually scores the most points on the team.

Kyrie Irving's ball-handling skills help him navigate around opponents to the basket.

Rebounders

A rebounder on the defense is usually a tall player who grabs opponents' missed shots, called defensive **rebounds**. When his or her team has the ball, the rebounder attempts a lot of shots and might score many points. A three-point rebounder excels at grabbing opponents' rebounds but is also a good ball handler. This player tends to attempt and make more three-point shots than other players.

Timeline of Basketball History

1891
Dr. James Naismith, an instructor at a YMCA in Springfield, Massachusetts, invents basketball.

1896
The first professional basketball game is played in Trenton, New Jersey.

Protectors

The players who strike the most fear in their opponents are called paint protectors. Paint protectors are often players who tower over their opponents. They easily block shots and pull down rebounds under the basket in the key. Some paint protectors may not score many points, and they tend to commit a lot of fouls. However, a scoring paint protector does it all: scores points, grabs rebounds, and blocks shots.

1949

The National Basketball League joins the Basketball Association of America to form the NBA.

1996

The Women's National Basketball Association (WNBA) is founded. The first WNBA game is played the following year.

The Winning Way

Alagappan's research also showed that successful NBA teams feature an assortment of players. A team with a mix of ball handlers and paint protectors, for example, is a balanced team with few weak spots. Weaker teams have too many players with similar skills. Alagappan's award-winning work may revolutionize the way professional and college basketball teams are assembled.

A well-balanced team can bring a group of players to victory.

Major Tournaments

The NBA and WNBA Finals are the associations' annual championship series. Each is played between the winners of the association's Western and Eastern **conferences**. The National Collegiate Athletic Association (NCAA) Finals is played each year between the United States' two top college teams. There is both a men's and a women's NCAA Finals championship. Basketball is also part of the Summer Olympics, which take place every four years. The team that wins the **tournament** receives gold medals (shown below).

Once a team scores,
the opposing team gets
possession of the ball.

Play Like the Pros

Being your best at basketball takes hard work. College and professional players spend hours each day practicing. With dedication, you can sharpen your skills to be the best you can be, too. Dribbling allows a player to move the ball past opponents to a new position. Strong passing techniques help teams move the ball quickly around the court. Being able to stop the opponent from scoring and being able to take possession of the ball are necessities on the defense.

Dribbling

As you dribble, keep the ball close and low to the ground, no higher than your waist. Push down on the ball with your fingertips and wrist, not the palms of your hands. Keep your head up, and "feel" the ball rather than look at it. Focus on the positions of your teammates and opponents, and on where you're moving. Once you stop dribbling, you cannot start again. You have to pass the ball to a teammate or try for a basket.

At first, practice dribbling while you are standing still.

Passing

A player can make a chest pass standing still or moving. Grip the ball with both hands, elbows tucked, at chest level. Look and step toward your teammate receiving the pass. Release the ball with a flick of the wrists and your arms straight. An overhead pass is usually done standing still.

Hold the ball with two hands above your head. Pass it with a snap of your wrists and fingers. To catch a pass, keep your eyes on the ball and use both hands.

A chest pass is one of the easiest passes to learn and use.

Shooting

There are many ways to make a basket. The two most common shots are the jump shot and the layup. To shoot a jump shot, start by facing the basket with your feet flat on the floor. Hold the ball level with your head and jump, looking directly at the basket. Your back and legs should be straight. At the peak of your jump, release the ball with a flick of the wrist toward the basket.

In a jump shot, your dominant hand (the one you write with) does most of the work.

You can do a layup on the move after catching a pass or when dribbling toward the basket. Get firm control of the ball in both hands as you approach the basket. Take off from the ground by jumping off the foot opposite your shooting hand. Stretch your arms up and take the hand opposite your shooting hand off the ball. Release the ball at the peak of your jump.

To shoot a layup, you'll need to get close to the basket.

Move with the person you're guarding.

Playing Defense

When playing defense, guard one player on the opposite team. Position yourself between that player and the basket. When guarding a dribbler, always face your opponent. Don't watch the ball or the person's eyes. He or she can use them to fake you out and make you move the wrong way. Focus on the person's waist instead. Keep your knees slightly bent and your feet shoulder-width apart. Shuffle your feet as you move to keep from tripping.

Grab a rebound to take possession of the ball for your team. Position yourself between the basket and your opponent with your back to the person. As the ball comes off the rim or backboard, jump toward it. Swing your arms and hands up to help lift you off the floor. With your arms up and hands ready, catch the ball. Quickly pass it to a teammate to begin your team's offensive attack.

Using your body to keep an offensive player from getting a rebound is called boxing out.

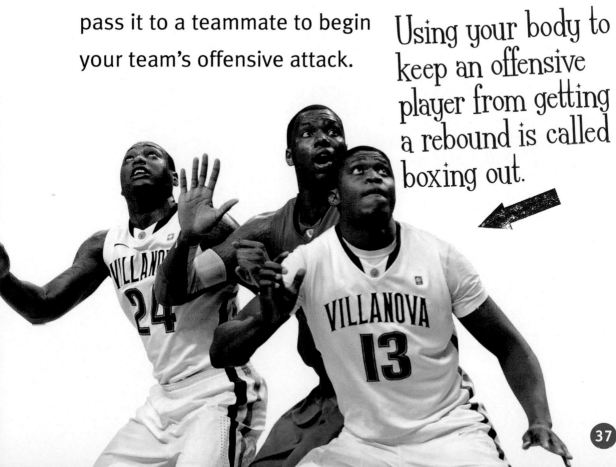

LeBron James of the Cleveland Cavaliers jumps to make a basket.

CHAPTER 6

Learn From the Legends

Professional basketball players are among the most gifted athletes in the world. Each one has practiced thousands of hours to become the best he or she can be. Of the thousands of players who have been in the NBA or WNBA, some stand head and shoulders above the rest. And there's always something a young basketball player can learn from these legendary players.

Jamming the ball through the basket from above is an exciting shot called a slam dunk.

Kareem Abdul-Jabbar is the NBA's career scoring leader with 38,387 points.

The Dominators

During his 15-season career, Wilt Chamberlain led the NBA in scoring seven times and in rebounding 11 times. Kareem Abdul-Jabbar was also a great scorer and rebounder. He perfected the graceful skyhook shot. Bill Russell was one of the NBA's greatest defensive players. His commitment to winning and teamwork earned him a record 11 NBA championships. Shaquille O'Neal, nicknamed Shaq, was famous for his backboard-rocking slam dunks.

The Shooters

Larry Bird wasn't the tallest or the strongest player, but he was a fierce competitor. Bird had the quickest jump shot release of anyone who ever played the game. He won the NBA Rookie of the Year award and was a three-time NBA champion.

Oscar Robertson had a huge range of talents. An outstanding defender and passer, "The Big O" could score from in close and from long range. His jump shot was picture-perfect.

Oscar Robertson

Oscar Robertson lands after making a layup for the Cincinnati Royals.

Michael Jordan became legendary during his career with the Chicago Bulls.

A Class by Themselves

Michael Jordan is the most famous basketball player of all time. "MJ" could do it all: shoot, pass, rebound, *and* defend. In his 15-season career, Jordan led the league in scoring 11 times. He won six NBA championships and five Most Valuable Player (MVP) awards.

Many people think LeBron James is the best player today. Strong, graceful, and quick, James is nearly unstoppable. He also has one of the finest jump shots in the league.

Women Basketball Stars

Playing for the U.S. women's basketball team, Diana Taurasi won three Olympic gold medals. Then on the Phoenix Mercury team of the WNBA, Taurasi won the Rookie of the Year and MVP awards. She is a five-time WNBA scoring champion and a three-time WNBA champion.

Lisa Leslie was one of women's basketball's most dominant players. She won four Olympic gold medals and three WNBA MVP awards. Leslie is also the league's all-time leader in rebounds. All of these players are great examples of being your best at basketball. ★

Diana Taurasi drives around an opponent toward the basket.

True Statistics

Size of a basketball used in the NBA: 22 oz. (623.7 g) with a 29.5 in. (75 cm) circumference

World's tallest basketball player ever: Suleiman Ali Nashnush of the national team of Libya, 8 ft. (2.4 m)

Shortest player in NBA history: Muggsy Bogues, 5 ft. 3 in. (1.6 m)

Most points scored in an NBA game by a single player: 100, by Wilt Chamberlain on March 2, 1962

Largest attendance at a basketball game: 108,713, at the 2010 NBA All-Star Game in Dallas, Texas

Number of Olympic gold medals won in basketball by the United States: 14 by the men's team, 7 by the women's

Player with the most games played in the NBA: Robert Parish, with 1,611

Did you find the truth?

F Basketball is a game played only by tall people.

T Basketball is played around the world.

Resources

Books

Kaplan, Bobby. *Bball Basics for Kids*. Bloomington, IN: iUniverse, 2012.

Sports Illustrated Kids Big Book of Who: Basketball. New York: Time Home Entertainment, 2015.

Visit this Scholastic Web site for more information on being your best at basketball:

★ www.factsfornow.scholastic.com
Enter the keywords **Being Your Best at Basketball**

Important Words

analysis (uh-NAL-i-sis) the careful examination of something in order to understand it

backboard (BAK-bord) the upright board behind a basketball hoop

conferences (KAHN-fur-uhns-ez) groups of sports teams, often below professional status

field goals (FEELD GOLZ) baskets made when the ball is in play, scoring two or three points

free throw (FREE THROW) an unguarded shot worth one point, taken from behind the free throw line; players get free throws when they are fouled

league (LEEG) a group of sports teams, usually professional

personal foul (PUR-suh-nuhl FOWL) a penalty called to prevent a player from gaining an advantage over an opponent; personal fouls usually involve physical contact

rebounds (REE-boundz) when missed shots bounce off the rim or backboard

tournament (TOOR-nuh-muhnt) a series of contests in which a number of people or teams try to win the championship

violation (vye-uh-LAY-shun) a breaking of the rules that causes a team to lose possession of the ball

Index

Page numbers in **bold** indicate illustrations.

About the Author

Nel Yomtov is an award-winning author with a passion for writing nonfiction books for young readers. He has written books and graphic novels about history, geography, science, and other subjects. Nel has worked at Marvel Comics, where he edited, wrote, and colored hundreds of titles. He has also served as editorial director of a children's book publisher and as publisher of Hammond World Atlas books.

Yomtov lives in the New York City area with his wife, Nancy, a teacher. Their son, Jess, is a sports journalist.